Losing Control

A Biblical Plan For Responding To Incarceration

Ruben Constante, Jr.

Your Voice Creations

ISBN (978-0-9980803-6-9)

2016, Ruben Constante, Jr., author
www.blueprintsflm.com
www.facebook.com/Blueprints-for-Living-Ministries

Cover design by Constante Photo
www.constantephoto.com

Printed in the United States of America

Published by Your Voice Creations
San Francisco, CA

To Desiree and Eric
because you two were hurt the most

CONTENTS

ACKNOWLEDGEMENTS

Many men were key in helping shape my understanding of God, His Word, and humanity. They were mentors, preaching partners, and men who held me accountable to remain a faithful steward of God's manifold grace.

Ted White, my first mentor. He served as a volunteer chaplain at the Bexar County Adult Detention Center.

Rudy Garcia, my first mentor in white. We met in 2004 during Kairos Walk #12 at the Torres Unit in Hondo, Texas.

Jason Cole, my first preaching partner. He was pivotal in providing my cerebral approach to Christianity the compassion it lacked.

Israel Garza, my first preaching "fall partner." He was the one who ran into my life when everyone seemed to run out.

Those four men were the most pronounced in my life, but there were others who influenced me as well: Moses Toribio, Robert Brandenburg, Amos De Leon, Javier Gaitan, Lorens San Pedro, and Guillermo Quinones. And then there were my first two "Rubenites," Joseph Sterling and Eriac Corley, the two disciples who sat daily with me to learn more of God's Word---and were ridiculed for following me so closely. (Much love to you two!)

Thank you all for putting up with me.

"For what I am doing, I do not understand. For what I will to do, that I do not practice; but what I hate, that I do."
Romans 7:15

Chapter One

WELCOME TO PRISON

You are about to read a short book on how to deal with incarceration. It will challenge everything you know about doing time. It will upset you. It will frustrate you. And you may even disagree with much of what's written in these short pages.

But nothing will change the fact that you are reading it.

What that means is God has a plan for you. He is drawing you right now to reconsider why you are incarcerated. You may have your own answers for why you are locked up. You may think that so and-so is responsible for your incarceration, and if it wasn't for them, you'd be free. Sadly, that kind of thinking is only making you serve some hard time!

Losing Control is written with the express purpose of helping you understand how you can deal with the real issues which led to your incarceration. Sure, you've broken the law, and that's why you've been apprehended and turned over to the custody of some correctional institution. But that's only the symptom of the problem. *You broke the law because something has been brewing within you.* It's been eating you up. You can't function well. You are always angry, frustrated, sad, or bitter.

It's controlling you.

That something is what this book is going to address. Short and to-the-point, it contains some reflective questions at the end of each chapter and a few scriptural readings for you to ponder. Read the questions. Answer them. They will address what's hidden beneath your hardened exterior. The scriptural readings provide you with biblical references to what each chapter discussed.

You're doing time. That's a fact. It's time you deal with the real reason why. It's time you put aside every excuse you've used to defend your wounded ego. It's time you set aside your vendetta against whomever you think is out to get you. It's time to get to the bottom of this problem you've created for yourself.

It's time to regain control!

You are now sitting in a jail or prison cell where millions of inmates before you have sat. You are wearing the same clothes they wore, eating the same food they did, and you're being told what to do by the same people who "bossed" them around.

It doesn't sound like much to be excited about does it? Of course, it doesn't! But you're here, and you're probably wondering how you can get yourself out of this mess. Whether you're in the county jail or in a state or federal prison, you wish you were home with your loved ones.

Been there done that, my friend. I served 18 years on a 20-year sentence, and not one day went by I didn't wish I'd have listened to those people who were warning me about the consequences of my foolish lifestyle. But I didn't. I was mistakenly convinced I had been in complete control of my life, that I didn't need anyone to give me advice or "tell me what to do." How wrong I had been!

The truth was I lost complete control of my life. And that's exactly where you find yourself today in a state of powerlessness. That's right: powerlessness. Incarceration has stripped you of the power to take a walk in the park or go out to eat at a restaurant or enjoy the company of your loved ones. And you're in that position because *you lost control of your life.*

The good news is you can regain rightful control over it, because you have plenty of time to rethink a few things about yourself. You have reflection time. In this sense, your incarceration is the best thing that has happened to you so far. You can discover who you truly are, because you don't have anything or anybody to distract you. You don't have your drugs, alcohol, cars, clothes, homes, or illicit relationships to identify with. You are now stripped of all those things and people who you allowed to give you a false identity, and now you can finally sit down and think about what direction in life you're travelling.

You can now regain control of your life!

This book is designed to help you understand why you *really* got locked up, how to "survive" while you're here, and what to do about the sinful issues which have controlled you up the this point. As you "do time," you are now able to search deeply within yourself to see what the root of your problem has been. In short, incarceration is a blessing in disguise.

You may not see light at the end of the tunnel, but if you give yourself a chance you will soon discover there is hope for you. Your reason for existing has not been erased by this incarceration. It has merely been distorted by it. But you can learn what the true reason is if you choose to follow the One who created you.

If you are reading this book, rest assured that God made a way for you to do so. He is calling you right now. He is hearing the cries of your soul. He knows you're angry, hurt, scared, and lonely. He knows.

So, if you want to learn about the process which is required to become the person you were meant to be, keep reading. If you want to learn why you got locked up, keep reading. If you want to experience hope in an otherwise hopeless situation, keep reading.

If you want to regain control of your life, turn the next page!

Chapter Two

CREATED FOR CONTROL

Human beings want a lot of things in life: money, jobs, relationships, etc. Additionally, all of us want to experience love, joy, peace, and happiness. And no matter how much difficulty life can bring us, most of us keep pressing forward, hoping tomorrow promises something better.

But of all that we desire, nothing is more basic to our human longings than the desire for self-preservation. We all want to live as long as we can. To achieve this, we engage in all manner of conflicts and wars to ensure the survival of ourselves, our clan, and/or our nation. What this drive to survive results in is an incessant quest for power and control. Where did this desire come from? It

came from a distorted stewardship handed to us
from God.

> " 'Then God said, 'Let Us make
> man in Our image. . .let them have
> dominion. . .' " (Gen. 1:26).

When God created us in His image, He entrusted
us with the responsibility of managing this planet.
We were given the right to rule over His creation.
We were given dominion. However, when dominion falls under the influence of sin and death, it
becomes a desperate craving for power and control. In a pre-fallen state, humans would rightfully
exercise rulership over planet Earth.

Under the curse of sin, we now distort that rulership and abuse it entirely. Instead of exercising
biblical rulership over God's non-human creation,
we are now under *its* power. Instead of us ruling
over the plant kingdom, for example, the plant
kingdom rules over us in the form of all the drugs
(legal or not) which we have allowed to subdue
the entire human race.

Plus, we now ruthlessly dominate other humans
in anyway we can. We were not created to rule over
one another, yet human experience proves that's
all we really want to do: rule over other members
of the human race. Sadly, we've taken God's design
of stewardship over His creation and transformed
it into a tyrannical mechanism to control others

in our lives. We've distorted its design and turned dominion into domination.

One of the first things you need to understand is that you have control issues. We all do, in fact. Each of us manages this problem differently. Some of us hurt ourselves and others with it, while others remain relatively civil and law-abiding about it. Either way, every person struggles with taming this desire for power and control.

However, what exactly does it mean to have "control issues"? Simply put, it means God's basic design for humans to exercise rulership is being twisted. It means you and I desire (even secretly!) to have others conform to our version of reality. We see this when we try to change people and "fix" them. We play God.

The other day while I was in an AA meeting which I must attend as a condition for my release from prison, I was listening to the facilitator of this particular meeting attempt to define what it meant to "play God." He tried his best but found himself visibly struggling with putting this issue into words. So I chimed in. After raising my hand, I said, "Trying to play God basically means that a person attempts to control people, situations, and outcomes." I paused for effect, watching heads nod in surprising agreement, and then I finished. "Playing God is all about power and control, for only God has all power and control. Sadly, we are born with the drive to *be* God instead submitting ourselves *to* Him---and we always get in trouble for it!"

When viewed this way, each of us has an issue with control. We just have different ways of expressing it. For us who know the incarcerated life by experience, control issues resulted in criminal activity. You must know, then, that we were not created to exercise power and control over others, but to exercise rightful rulership over ourselves and what God has entrusted to our care.

The key to unlocking this awesome potential, however, depends on whether we understand how being created in God's image is directly connected to this divine responsibility.

> *" 'Then God said, 'Let Us make*
> *man in Our image. . .let them have*
> *dominion. . .' " (Gen. 1:26).*

We were created to rule in accordance with God's image. He gave us dominion to rule as He rules. Therefore, to know how we must exercise rightful rulership in our lives, we must consider how He rules:

> *"Righteousness and justice are the*
> *foundation of Your throne; mercy*
> *and truth go before Your face" (Ps.*
> *89:14).*

"Clouds and darkness surround Him; righteousness and justice are the foundation of His throne" (Ps. 97:2).

God rules in righteousness. God does nothing unrighteously. He exercises complete rule over everything according to His holy nature. "The Lord is righteous in all His works" (Ps. 145:17). Are we?

God is just in all He does. Moses wrote that God is "the Rock, His work is perfect; for all His ways are justice, a God of truth and without injustice; righteous and upright is He" (Deut. 32:4). Are we?

God is merciful in His rule. Psalm 103:10 says, "He has not dealt with us according to our sins, nor punished us according to our iniquities." Are as merciful with others as He is with us?

God rules in truth. Jesus said He is truth (Jn 14:6); therefore, everything God does is done in truth. Nothing erroneous issues from the godhead. Only truth. How often are we truthful?

As we see, we are a long way from ruling our lives the way God rules His universe. Yet, as His image bearers, we are called to reflect that type of rule. We are to be imitators of God (Eph. 5:1).

As you begin your journey as an inmate, make it your aim to become who God has called you to be. Incarceration isn't the end of the world; it's only the end of your sinful lifestyle---if you choose it. The following chapters are going to help you understand why you are locked and what you can about it.

Are you ready?

Questions for Reflection

1.What is the one thing you have trouble letting go of?

2.What do you think that says about you?

3.You were born to rule over God's non-human creation, not other humans. Is there someone you've been dominating?

4.What do you think has caused you to act this way toward them?

5.What steps can you take to release your grip over them?

Scriptural Readings

Proverbs 4:23	Matt. 12:33-37	Gal. 5:16-25
Proverbs 25:28	Matt. 15:19	

Chapter Three

ARRESTED ATTENTION

Ok, so now that you're here, what are you supposed to do? Now that your attention has been arrested, what happens next? Without a doubt, you are experiencing all kind of frustration, anger, anxiety, fear, and sadness. Those are perfectly normal reactions to being incarcerated. The challenge, however, is how to manage them. How do you regain control of your life?

Right now you may be thinking that if enough money is sent to you or if you get enough visits or if enough mail is sent to you, then your soul will be calmed. It won't. You're believing those things will help, because you (like the rest of us) have been conditioned to believe that happiness is achieved by how many things you have in your life or by how many relationships you are involved in. Those things are important to us---yes---but they are not what ultimately should define us.

And here's where incarceration serves as a blessing in disguise: It strips you of all those things and people you believed were responsible for fulfilling you and making you happy. All your life you've held others responsible for your happiness, and when they didn't make you happy, you reacted harshly. You lost your cool. You got high. You got drunk. You cheated on your spouse.

You blamed others for your bad response to their behavior.

In Christ, however, we are taught that being separated from those things and people which confer onto us a false identity is a good thing. Being locked up, it turns out, is God reminding you that the choices you've been making are keeping you away from Him, and the more you are separated from God the more you will come to ruin. So, yes, being separated from society right now is a good thing.

The Bible speaks clearly to the need for us to be separated from things and people who harm our relationship with Him. Therefore, the more you are separated from those things which separate you from Him, the more you are able to identify what those things are and why they are present in your life

It's time to identify what has been separating you from God! It's time to rethink your game plan for life. There are plenty of ways you can do this, but before we get to the root of it all, let's focus on the concept of separation, and then you'll get a fuller understanding of why you're locked up.

You were born separated from God

The Bible teaches that all us of were born sinners (Ps. 51:3; 58:3; Is. 48:8; Rom. 5:12). When God had told Adam not to eat of the Tree of the Knowledge of Good and Evil, He made it very clear why: because death awaited him on the other side of that bite (cf. Gen. 2:16-17). Death, however, doesn't mean a person ceases to exist. In Scripture, death means *separation*. When God had told Adam he would surely die, He meant more than anything else that Adam would be separated from His Creator.

In fact, there are three types of death which the Bible speaks of: spiritual, physical, and eternal. When Adam and Eve partook of the forbidden fruit, they instantly died *spiritually*. They were separated from God. What that meant was that they instantly lost their intimate communion with God. And they felt that absence very painfully in their soul---that's why they ran and hid (cf. Gen. 3:7-8).

Well, the same thing happens to us when we are separated from God. We are filled with shame and guilt, and we do everything we can to cover it up. To mask it. This is basically why people do drugs, drink alcohol, and why they do anything else to numb their soul pain They are trying to cover up their spiritual nakedness the same way Adam and Eve had tried to cover theirs.

Because we all born separated from God, we all try to cover up that inner nakedness with anything that promises to numb our soul pain. From the cradle to the grave, humans are engaged in a relentless quest to cover their spiritual nakedness. Bottom line: We are all born separated from God, and we do all we can to substitute His presence in our lives with whatever it is we think will take His place in our hearts.

Separation from God produces a separation from self

Because we are created in the image of God, our true identity as human beings can only be rightly understood when we reconnect with Him. There is so much scientific literature nowadays that tells us about how people can go through an "identity crisis" or have a "gender identity disorder" or that they can have a "bipolar disorder." But those psychological labels take the attention away from the real problem. Left to themselves, those labels brainwash people to believe the solution to their disorder is to ingest whatever antipsychotic drug is available on the market.

However, at the core of all those so-called disorders is a human spirit---a naked one---which is crying to be reconnected with its Creator. Our *spiritual* problems can only be corrected in *spiritual* ways. Sadly, though, many people (even Christians!) believe that psychiatry is the solution to the problems of the human heart. Well, here's a newsflash: *All the emotional and mental problems people experience are the direct result of being separated from God.*

This separation from God, then, produces a separation from self. Once a separation from self occurs, all manner of "disorders" begin to surface. When people are paranoid or anxious or depressed or whatever, they are experiencing a detachment from themselves. They don't know who they are anymore. They're lost.

Separation from self produces a separation from others

Broken relationships are seen everywhere: church splits, divorces, friendship betrayals, parent-child disputes, etc. Humans are always subject to relational conflict. It's human nature. The reason for this is because of the inner separation we are plagued with.

Interpersonal conflict is always the result of inner-personal conflict, and inner-personal conflict is always the result of being separated from God.

We must all get serious about how separation from God affects not only how we relate with ourselves, but how we relate with others. Being separated from God is a matter of life and death! It produces guilt, shame, fear, anxiety, depression, paranoia, etc. And when we don't return to Him for an authentic connection with Him, we always make matters worse.

Here's the raw truth: You are incarcerated because you have been living a lie. You've been pursuing a lifestyle (whatever it may be) in a subconscious attempt to reconnect your spirit to God. No matter where you worked, who you hung out with, how you passed your free time, or how many people you've been sexually involved with, everything you were doing was out of a deep-seated attempt to find fulfillment for your soul, not knowing your true fulfillment can only be found in reconnecting with God. You are sitting in that cell---separated from your family---because you've been living separated from God.

The question is: Are you ready to reconnect with Him?

Questions for Reflection

1. What are some of the things you know have separated you from God?

2. Are those things out of your life now that you're incarcerated?

3. Now take a deep look within your heart: What issues are you battling with and how are they separating you from God.

4. What relationship are you worried about losing most at this time? Why?

Scriptural Readings

Psalm 37:4-8	Psalm 39	Psalm 51
Luke 15:11-32	John 15:1-5	Rom. 12:9-21
Rom. 6:12-16	1 John 3:13-15	1 John 4:17-21

Chapter Four

———

NOW THAT YOU'RE HERE...

So far we have learned four things:

1. We were created in God's image,

2. We were created to exercise dominion,

3. We were were born separated from God, and

4. Being separated from God is the root cause of all the problems we get into.

To reiterate the main point here, you are incarcerated because you've been separated from God. On the surface, everyone will say you are locked up because of some crime you committed, and while that may be true the real reason why you are here is because *you have been disconnected from God.* Logically, then, the answer to avoid living like this any longer is for you to reconnect with Him. Only He can grant you the Holy Spirit Who will empower you with *true* control: the fruit of self-control. Only God can teach you how to steward your dominion; only He can show you how to rule your passions and how to live in right relation with others.

In the Old Testament, God had told His people they were being destroyed for a lack of knowledge (Hos. 4:6), and the same can be said for us today. Our world offers many options for living a good life or on how to cope with its harsh realities. "Try this lifestyle," says one person. "Take these pills," says some doctor. "Read this book," says some friend. "Life is short so live it up," says society. There are many people dispensing advice on how to live life, but if their counsel isn't taken from the blueprint of Scripture then it's meaningless and ultimately futile.

The truth is, no one can appropriately guide you into living a truly meaningful life because they didn't create you. They didn't design you. Only God can do that. He encoded within you a desire for relationship, a relationship only He can teach you how to cultivate. He created you for connection with Himself, and as long as you remain disconnected from Him you will continue to live a self-destructive life.

So now that you're incarcerated, it's time to look deeply at what you've been running from and what you've been running to. Here, we will cover a few points that may be of help.

What are you running from?

Everyone runs the rat race. We all want to strive for the best. We want to be loved, have power, own possessions, be accepted, be happy, etc. Nothing is inherently wrong with these things, for God Himself told Joshua that if he would meditate on God's Word and obey it without reserve, he would "make [his] way prosperous, and then you will have good success" (Jos. 1:8).

Did you notice God said Joshua *himself* would make his way prosperous? Yes, God has empowered us with free choice. He doesn't make us do anything. The power to succeed lies within our ability to choose. We experience success and happiness *as a result of choosing to obey God's Word.* We are directly responsible for making our own way prosperous and successful!

However, as we attempt to do that, we often *run from* the very things God has designed to fulfill us. For example: If a person works two or three jobs, they may not necessarily be wanting to only pay bills. Sometimes people work excessive hours, because they don't want to spend time with loved ones. They don't want to be at home. Maybe they are running from issues at home they don't know how to handle, so instead of slowing down and addressing those problems, they consume themselves with work. They use work as an excuse to *run from* dealing with problems at home.

This idea of *running from* problems never helps the person who is running. Running from problems only intensifies them. Imagine if you were diagnosed with cancer. You panic and don't know what to do. The doctor tells you it's in its early phase and it's not too late to treat it. However, you refuse to deal with. You don't want to admit to yourself or to anyone you have it. You don't want to be embarrassed perhaps. Either way, you don't seek the treatment you need. *You run from it. And the cancer kills you.*

Many times we do the same thing with our personal problems. We foolishly deny they exist, perhaps because we are too proud to admit we might have a particular weakness. Maybe we're just too stubborn to ask for help. Whatever the reason may be, we *run from the problem*. What's interesting about this approach is that we convince ourselves it's ok because we remain occupied with all sort of activity (even with lots of church attendance!). Here's the problem with that: Some of the most noticeable runners are people who are involved with too many activities and programs and spend little time with people in any meaningful way.

Runners are good at playing hide-n-seek.

Jesus once told a true story of a woman named Martha who was like that. She was an industrious woman and probably cooked and cleaned ten times better than most of us today! However, at the root of her "ministry" was a was wounded heart. Jesus exact words to her were: "Martha, Martha, you are worried and troubled about many things" (Lk. 10:41). He saw right through her service.

Busy bees are usually the fastest runners.

So now that you're here, ask yourself a few questions: *What am I running from? What don't I want to confront? Who am I afraid to talk to? Who I am afraid to become vulnerable with? What I am not wanting to deal with?*

What are you running to?

When Adam and Eve discovered they were naked, they ran, remember? They felt the shame and guilt of being disconnected from God, and they ran in fear. Instead of owning up to their sin and going to God about it, they ran to the bushes (cf. Gen. 3:8-10).

Whenever we are confronted with a problem, we either deal with it, deny it, or delay it. When we deal with it, we hit it head-on. We address the heart issues that underlie our problem, not just what's happening on the outside. When we deny it, that's when we run. We pretend the problem isn't there and secretly hope it will go away or that someone else will deal with. When we delay it, we admit the problem exists, but we procrastinate. We put it off for another day (again, secretly hoping it will go away!). Delaying always makes matters worse.

In running from our problems we oftentimes run to temporary fixes. For example: If you are running from a broken relationship with your spouse, you might find yourself running to another partner. If you are running from a divorce, you might find yourself running to alcohol. If you are running from the loss of a job, you might find yourself running to drugs. If you are running from the fear of rejection, you might find yourself in isolation.

There can be a million things we run from, and in each instance there are a million other things waiting for us to run to, things that drive us further away from the healing our wounded heart needs. In short, when we run from God we run into more trouble.

Think about the way you've been living. What lifestyle have you been pursuing? Who have you been hanging around with? How did you manage to make money? All the things we do when running from God *always* get us into more problems. So now that you're here, locked up and away from your loved ones, take some time to re-evaluate yourself. Consider this a privilege most people don't have. Remember: You used to be one of those people, running from God and running to everything else for comfort and connection!

Take some time to acknowledge that you are running and *have been* running all your life. You are reading this book by divine providence. God made sure you would read it because He loves you. He wants you to live a fulfilled life, a life characterized by connection. But you have to come to terms with the fact that you've been living separated from Him. Realize that you've been hurting yourself and others around you. You may think you weren't really hurting anybody because perhaps you weren't doing anything particularly dangerous or weren't committing any violent crimes, but you must remember that just as there is no such thing as a "victimless crime," there is no such thing as a *harmless* disconnection from God. Every time you run from God someone gets hurt. *What are you running to in an attempt to find relief from your pain? Who are you running to as a distraction from your troubled heart?*

These are real questions you must confront and answer. As the saying goes: "You can run, but you can't hide." So why not come out from the bushes and listen to the words of Jesus? He said, "Come to Me, all you who labor and are heavy laden, and I will give you rest" (Matt. 11:28). Aren't you tired of running, my friend? Aren't you exhausted with all the games you've been playing? Jesus has a place in His heart for you. He has the perfect rest for your troubled soul.

Now that you're here,
will you run to Jesus?

Questions for Reflection

1.Mediate on this for a moment: What issue have you been avoiding?

2.And now think carefully about this: What things have you been doing to avoid it?

3.In conclusion, what problems have you created by running from that problem you've been avoiding?

4.What steps can you take (beginning right now!) to deal with that issue you've been running from?

Scriptural Readings

Genesis 3	Proverbs 13:20	Ephesians 5
Jonah 1	Proverbs 14:7	Heb. 12:3-11
Psalm 1	1 Cor. 15:33	James 1:12-15

Chapter Five

RIGHTFUL REIGN

We've come to the end of ourselves, haven't we? Those of us who have experienced incarceration know very well what that means! Getting locked up can feel like the end of the world. It feels like nothing and no one can help you feel better about it. And honestly, in a very real sense, no one can help you. Not even *you* can help yourself.

> *"Then Jesus said, 'If anyone desires*
> *to come after Me. . ." (Matt. 16:24a).*

Let's stop right there for a moment. Do you remember just a few minutes ago that we learned about Jesus' invitation to give us soul rest? After all the back-breaking, soul-wrenching labor we've endured for so many years, running here and there trying to find fulfillment with God---after all the dead ends we've run into---Jesus simply says, "Come here, my child. I want to give you rest." What an awesome invitation! Yet that rest He promises isn't an easy way out of your problems. Jesus absolutely guarantees He'll give you rest, but not without a price. .

". . .let him deny himself, and take
up his cross, and follow Me"
(Matt. 16:24b).

Okay, let's stop again, because these words are profound. Our disconnection from God has weighed heavy on us. All our lives we've been trying to find completeness, yet in our maddening search we only developed some really bad habits of coping with an unfulfilled soul. All of us have done this. We've attempted to mend our broken hearts, but in every attempt that didn't include an intimate encounter with God through Jesus Christ, we found ourselves with more pain.

Thankfully, God hasn't left us to fend for ourselves. He's provided a way for us to finally reconnect with Him, and that path is through a rugged cross. So here's the secret to obtaining the rest our souls long for:

denying ourselves those hurtful
ways we've used to cope with being
separated from God.

Yes, my friend. It's that simple. Simple, but not easy, I know. Whatever you've been doing to find fulfillment, refrain from doing that. Whatever you've been doing to reconnect with God, stop it. It hasn't worked---and it never will.

"Denying yourself" is a popular Christian phrase, but it has been widely misunderstood. It doesn't mean withholding from yourself those basic element your body needs to survive, nor does it mean avoiding loving relationships with people (something God created you for in the first place!). Denying yourself means you stop running from God and that you stop running to the bushes. It means you stop trying to fabricate homemade clothes to cover your spiritual nakedness. Adam and Eve sewed fig leaves together to cover themselves, but those coverings weren't good enough (Gen. 3:7, 21).

And they aren't good enough to cover yours either.

Listen: We all do things to cope with spiritual nakedness (our separation from God) by covering ourselves with this or that, but we have to admit that every time we do that we push ourselves farther away from the only Person who can truly cover us and make us whole. "Denying yourself" means you stop trying to reconnect with God on your terms. But wait! Jesus isn't through preaching here. . .

*"For whoever desires to save his life
will lose it, but whoever loses his life
for My sake will find it"
(Matt. 16:25).*

So this is what all your attempts to reconnect with God have really been about: *self-preservation*. It's no secret we live in a hostile world; people are robbed, hurt, lied to, killed, injured, cheated on, betrayed, and even killed.

Our fallen, sinful natures which we inherited from Adam have produced a million ways for us to cope with our separation from God, and each one of them has resulted in pain and suffering for ourselves and for others. We've created a jungle out of a garden, and everyone is doing all they can to survive that jungle. Everyone is trying *to save themselves.*

Yet Jesus said that in resorting to all those earthly ways of "saving" ourselves, we've actually lost our way. Instead of saving our lives, we've lost them. The more we try to save our life---as Jesus put it---the more we lose it. Our efforts are fruitless, because nothing we do on our own can reconnect us with God. We were born separated from God and all our lives we've fought tooth-and-nail to push away the pain which that separation has caused us. We've been trying to save our lives, and we've only managed to lose them even more.

Now let's bring this whole thing right back to where we started. It's just you alone in that jail cell, thinking about where it all went wrong for you.

Well, my friend, you may conclude that you are locked up because you did this or didn't do that; or, you may think you are facing a lengthy prison sentence sentence because you weren't smart enough to break the law without getting caught. All the reasons you may come up with might be true and offer a shallow explanation for why you are locked up, but beneath it all lies the true reason for why is all went wrong:

You were born separated from God.

Because of this separation, you experienced spiritual nakedness, and that nakedness drove you in a lifelong search to be clothed; you've been looking for fulfillment and for anything that would give you the illusion of being covered. Anything that would make you feel good.

In reality, though, those things you thought were covering you were only creating a wider gap between you and God, the only One who can clothe you.

When He created you, He placed within you the right to rule---to take control of His creation. But instead of ruling as you were created to rule, you became overruled by everything and everyone around you! You became a slave to your passions (lust, pride, anger, etc.). You were dominated by things which weren't designed to overtake you.

As a result of being enslaved to your passions, you lost control and broke the law, and now you're hoping someone will make your bond and get you out of the mess you've created for yourself. But think about this for a moment: If someone did bail you of jail, what has really changed about you? If you got out right now, would those things that dominated you remain your master? If so---and I think they are!---then you would serve no one any good by getting out. You'd just make matters worse. (Trust me: I've been there, done that!)

So in all of this, you were never really in control of anything. You have been living your life separated from God, doing all you can to feel good about your spiritual nakedness, but in the process you developed some bad habits which became your taskmaster. You were a slave to them. Bottom line: *You were never in control.*

> *"And you [God] made alive, [you]*
> *who were dead in trespasses and*
> *sins. . .fulfilling the desires of the*

*flesh and of the mind, [you] were by
nature [a child] of wrath"
(Eph. 2:1-3).*

Because you were born a sinner (like every one of
us in the human race), *you were completely under
the control of your sinful nature.* You were born
with the ability to freely choose (a.k.a. "free will"),
but that power to choose was under the bondage
of sin.

Your free will was only as free as you are now.
As an inmate you can freely do what you want in
your cell, but that tiny enclosure restricts what
you can do. Therefore, you aren't truly "free."
You're only able to move wherever you're allowed
to move.

Same thing happens to our free will. We are
free to choose what we want to do, but we can't
break free of sin's confining power. Our ability to
choose is on lockdown to sin's death grip over our
soul. So, from day one of your existence, you were
never in control of anything, because your sinful
nature was controlling you! What a humbling fact!

However, God wants you to exercise rightful
authority in your life; He wants you back in control, so to speak. Not in the sense of you doing
whatever you want independent of submitting to
His authority, but in the sense of you regaining
what the devil stole from you in the beginning.

God desires that you live freely and for you to enjoy the abundant life He promises you in Christ Jesus. Why? Because He created you to exercise dominion. He created to exercise self-control.

In that sense, He wants you in control: of your senses, your emotions, and your decision making.

Think about this for a moment: God created us to exercise self-control and to rule His creation, but the reality is that we have lost self-control and are dominated by God's creation. Instead of us taking charge, we are being charged. How many times have you surrendered your decision-making power to the influence of some mind-altering substance? How many times have you allowed something or someone to steal your cool?

You see it now? We haven't really been in control, have we? We've been under the influence of our sinful nature and of the desires of our flesh (cf. Gal. 5:24).

Dear friend, the time has come for you to reconnect with God. It's time to regain your rightful reign. And it begins by surrendering yourself to the Lordship of Jesus Christ. He died to set you free from sin's powerful control over your life. He came to earth to reconnect you to God. To clothe your spiritual nakedness and fulfill your heart's desires. If you are tired of running from God and running to more problems, and if you want to regain true control of your life, then talk to Him right now. It doesn't have to be some fancy prayer.

Just tell Him how you feel. Tell Him you're scared and lonely. Tell Him you need help. Admit that you've been living your life trying to reconnect with Him on your own terms and that you now realize it was wrong. Just look at the criminal's confession in Luke 23: 40-42, and you'll see that Jesus hears a convict's cry.

And He's waiting to hear yours.

Questions for Reflection

1. In what ways have you lost control of your life?

2. Name five things (or people) who you now realize have been dominating you.

3. We just learned that we were never really in control of our lives, because our sinful natures were the driving force to all that we did. Our free will was under the bondage of sin and no matter what we did we couldn't save ourselves. Write down how you've been trying to save yourself all these years.

4. Finally, what are you willing to deny yourself today in an effort to reconnect with God and receive the healing your soul desires?

Scriptural Readings

Jer. 2:11-13	Eze. 22:17-22	Romans 12:1-2
Jer. 2:17-19	Daniel 9:3-19	Phil. 3:12-14
Lam. 3:1-42	Matt. 11:28-30	Phil. 4:6-8

CONCLUSION

Well, here we are at the end of our reading. And guess what, my friend? You still have no control over what is going to happen to you regarding the judicial system! Your loved ones are still out there and so are all your material possessions. Why am I reminding you of the obvious? To help you understand that your legal situation has absolutely nothing to do with your walk with the Lord. As you begin to grow in Christ and mature in His Word, the judicial system will not magically bow down to you and let you go home.

> *Coming to Christ does not cancel a consequence.*

The good news, however, is that you are now prepared to begin a new chapter in your life and get on the right track. Throughout this book, you were given ax-to-the-root information on why you got locked up and how you can best avoid that from ever happening again. And you are now placed in a position to receive the healing your heart desperately needs.

All that's required of you at this moment is to make a decision. Hopefully, you've surrendered yourself over to the care and control of God and you will begin to draw closer to Him in prayer, Bible reading, and fellowship with other believers. The Bible says He created you to rule (to exercise dominion and have self-control), and the only way to do that according to your design is for you to return to Him.

Don't let others discourage you from going to the source of Life. Don't let false ideas of God keep you from receiving a new life worth living. God doesn't command us to live holy simply because He wants us to live boring lives. *His commands are not restrictive but protective in nature.* You don't impose rules on your children because you want to prevent them from having fun. No, you impose guidelines for them to abide by because you want to protect them. Your "rules" are for their good.

God has done the same thing for us. When He had told Adam to not eat of the forbidden fruit, He wasn't doing it to be mean. It was for Adam's own good. God knew that sin would separate Adam from Him; therefore, telling Adam not to eat of the Tree of the Knowledge of Good and Evil was designed to *protect Adam's relationship with God*. And God wants to protect His relationship with you, too!

Consider this time you are spending in jail as

an opportunity to reconnect with Him. He didn't create you to live in such an abnormal place like that. He created you for freedom.

The problem is that you have been living a lie, thinking that whatever it is that you were doing out in the free world was the good life. There is nothing good about living separated from God. So now is the time, my friend. Protect yourself and those you love by *protecting your relationship with God*. There is simply no other way of regaining control of your life.

The choice is yours!